ROBERT QUACKENBUSH

THE BOY WHO DREAMED OF ROCKETS

HOW ROBERT H. GODDARD BECAME THE FATHER OF THE SPACE AGE

PARENTS' MAGAZINE PRESS · NEW YORK

For Piet

and with warmest good wishes to
Mrs. Robert H. Goddard

Library of Congress Cataloging in Publication Data

Quackenbush, Robert M.
The boy who dreamed of rockets.

SUMMARY: A biography of the American physicist responsible for many of the underlying principles of modern rocketry. Includes instructions for a model multistage rocket and an explanation of rocket flight.
1. Goddard, Robert Hutchings, 1882–1945—Juvenile literature. 2. Rocketry—United States—Biography—Juvenile literature. [1. Goddard, Robert Hutchings, 1882–1945. 2. Physicists. 3. Rocketry] I. Title.
TL781.85.G6Q32   629.4′092′4 [B] [92]78-21882
ISBN 0-8193-0995-8   ISBN 0-8193-0996-6 lib. bdg.

❧ PROLOGUE ☙

"And the rocket's red glare,
The bombs bursting in air,
Gave proof thro' the night
That our flag was still there."

These words from the national anthem of the United States, written by Francis Scott Key, mention the powder-fueled rocket missiles used during the British bombardment of Fort McHenry in 1814. Rockets like these, descendants of the 3000-year-old Chinese skyrockets still used in firework displays, were believed to have nearly reached their limit of development. Then along came an American physicist and engineer, born in Massachusetts in 1882, who set out to disprove this idea and to launch science into modern rocketry and the dawning of the Space Age. His name was Robert Hutchings Goddard.

1887 · FIVE-YEAR-OLD ROBERT ATTEMPS TO SOAR INTO SPACE.

There was once a boy named Robert Goddard, who liked anything that had to do with science. Robert had no brothers or sisters to play with, but it wasn't a problem for him. He had no trouble thinking of things to do. From an early age, he read science magazines and tried many imaginative experiments. His earliest experiment was when he was five. He learned that scuffing his feet across a carpet could produce sparks. He also learned how a battery stored electricity. He thought if he combined the two effects he could send himself soaring into space. So one day he went outside and scuffed his feet on the gravel walk. Then, holding a part of an old battery in one hand, he climbed a low fence and jumped. He fell to the ground with a thud! That ended that particular experiment, but it was not the last of Robert's scientific pursuits by any means.

Robert tried all kinds of scientific experiments when he was growing up. He even built his own frog hatchery with complicated motors and wheels to pump water into the frog's shelter. Robert's inventiveness may have stemmed from the fact that many of his ancestors were machinists. Even his father was a manufacturer and inventor of machine tools. Aside from this, whatever Robert did he always received support and encouragement from his parents. His grandmother, who lived in the home, also encouraged him. If there was an accident such as a broken window as a result of one of Robert's experiments, she would say, "Oh, it's just Robert experimenting again."

With all the experiments Robert did, he never lost sight of what gripped him the most: the science of flight and of space. He aimed arrows to the sky that he made with specially weighted wire tips to make them fly higher. He built and tested all kinds of kites. One amazing kite was to be a permanent balloon that would require no refilling. It was made from a sheet of aluminum that Robert tried to fill with lighter-than-air hydrogen gas so he could launch it high over Boston. Unfortunately, the kite was too heavy to leave the ground. "Failior crowns enterprise," Robert wrote in the diary he kept on his experiments. He was too discouraged to care that he had misspelled "failure."

1895 · ROBERT SHOOTS ARROWS 300 FEET IN THE AIR

When Robert was sixteen, he was struck with a kidney ailment. He had to drop out of school. During his recovery, two things happened to Robert that were to shape and change his whole life. The first was his reading of a science fiction book called "Fighters from Mars or The War of the Worlds" by the space prophet H. G. Wells, which made a strong impression on him. The second was a daydream.

Robert never forgot the day of his dream. It was October 19, 1899. He had climbed a cherry tree near his house. Up in the tree, he imagined he was in a spaceship. He looked at the ground below and imagined he saw such a device suddenly rise from the ground, zoom past him, and go soaring upward into space. Afterwards, Robert felt that he was, in his own words, "a different boy." He now had a goal in life. The goal was to invent the device he had imagined. But he knew that if such a device were to be discovered—or invented—it would be the result of knowledge of physics and mathematics. So he began at once by assigning himself a mass of hard reading and by keeping a file marked "Aerial Navigation Department."

1899 · ROBERT HAS A VISION OF THE FUTURE IN A CHERRY TREE

1905 · ON INDEPENDENCE DAY ROBERT WATCHES SKYROCKETS

Robert was nineteen before he was well enough to go back to school and finish three years of high school. He amazed his teachers with his great knowledge of science. They encouraged him to write articles and to send them to publishers. One article, entitled "The Navigation of Space", was a proposal to send several cannons skyward. The cannons would be arranged like a "nest" of beakers. Each cannon, when fired, would eject a lighter one, with the uppermost cannon, or "payload", traveling to great altitudes—just as our modern step or multistage rockets do today. This article, as well as the others, was rejected by the publishers. Robert's thinking was ahead of his time. Travel to outer space? Impossible! But Robert was not discouraged. He kept on with his dream. In a speech to his graduating class, he ended by saying, "The dream of yesterday is the hope of today and the reality of tomorrow."

When he graduated from high school, Robert went on to attend Worcester Polytechnic Institute. One summer, he suddenly knew what the device of his dreams was to be. It came to him when he was watching a fireworks display one Independence Day and saw skyrockets streaming across the sky. That is when he knew that the device was to be a rocket.

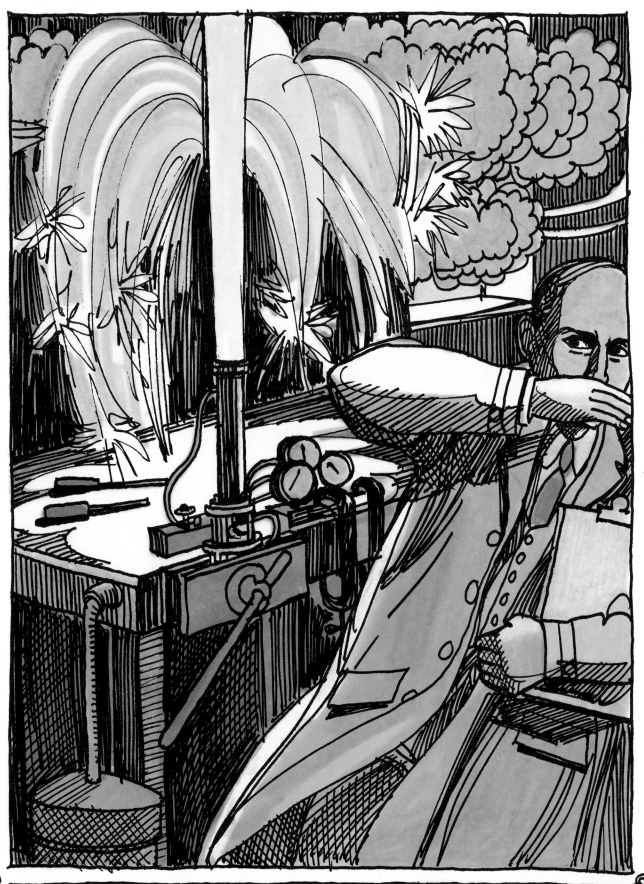

1911 · DR. GODDARD TESTS SOLID-FUEL ROCKETS AT CLARK

In 1908, Robert received his first science degree. Three years later, he received a doctorate from Clark University in Worcester, Massachusetts. He was now Doctor Robert Hutchings Goddard. He stayed on at Clark as a noted professor of physics. In his free hours, Dr. Goddard began rocket experiments in the laboratory at Clark. He tested many kinds of solid-fuel rockets that used powder fuels like gunpowder—the only kind of fuels being used in rockets at the time. Many times the noise of the explosions and the smoke pouring from the laboratory made the fire alarm go off. "Oh, it's just Dr. Goddard experimenting again," everybody would say.

After testing many rockets, Dr. Goddard was sure solid fuels would not be of any use in space research. A liquid-fuel rocket was his answer. Higher speeds could be attained with liquid fuels. They would be easier to control; the burning of the fuel could be turned on and off in flight. Liquid fuels would also allow the rocket's engine to work better and more smoothly. Knowing this, Dr. Goddard believed the ideal combination would be liquid hydrogen and liquid oxygen—with the liquid oxygen, or lox, supporting the burning in the airlessness of space. The two fuels would burn furiously together, and the expanding gases, as a result, would thrust the rocket upward. But these "fuels of the future" were not yet available. So Dr. Goddard had to settle for improving the performance and design of the solid fuel rocket until they were available.

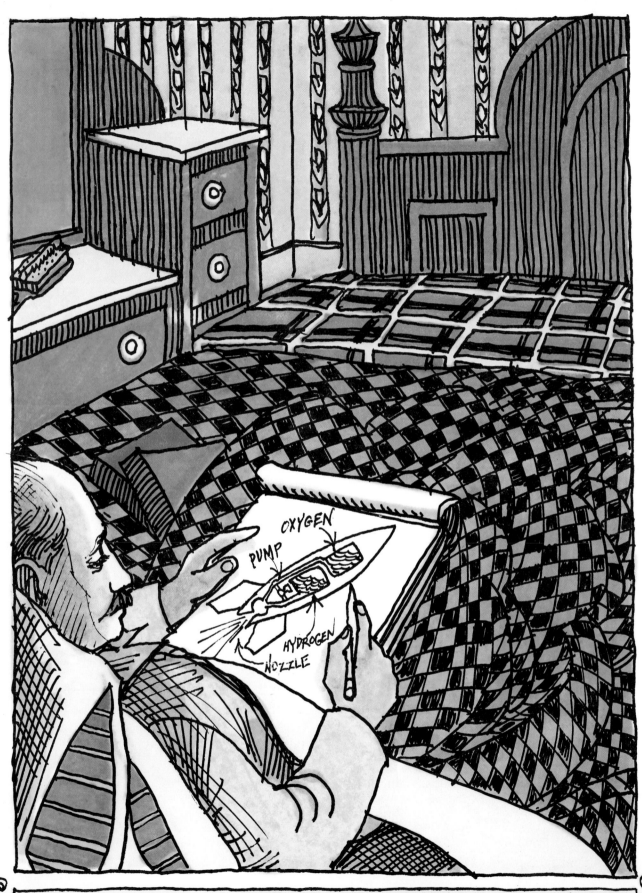

1914 · THOUGH ILL, DR· GODDARD STILL KEEPS ON WITH HIS WORK

In 1912, Dr. Goddard was offered a teaching position at Princeton University, which he gladly accepted. There he worked long hours in the laboratory, involved in a number of delicate experiments. The doors and windows, even the keyholes of the laboratory had to be sealed, because the slightest current of air or change in air temperature could throw off the precise measurements. Because of this, Dr. Goddard was constantly breathing bad fumes from the gas machinery with which he was working. It was no wonder he developed a racking cough, which he couldn't shake. After only a year at Princeton, he went home to Worcester with a second major illness—tuberculosis. Though the doctors thought he would die, he got better. He was determined to live and to go on with his research.

During his long recovery in bed, Dr. Goddard allowed himself an hour a day with his notes, which he kept under his pillow. Eventually he decided to have some of his rocket ideas patented. His patents covered three basic concepts of rocketry. The first had to do with the rocket's combustion (fuel-burning) chamber and its nozzle for letting out the escaping gases. The second had to do with a system for pumping fuel, both liquid and solid, to the combustion chamber. And the third was his idea for a step, or multistage rocket.

At last Dr. Goddard was well enough to go back to work. He taught part time at Clark and devoted the rest of his time to continue his rocket experiments. One of his new experiments was to prove, against the belief of scientific experts of the day, that a rocket could travel in the airlessness of space. Dr. Goddard did this by firing a pistol in the air and measuring how far the pistol kicked back, or recoiled. Then he fired the pistol in an airless chamber and measured how far the pistol recoiled. To his great satisfaction, he saw that the recoil was greater in the airless chamber than in ordinary air. It was proof that if a rocket with the right fuel got beyond the earth's atmosphere, it would be able to fly even faster in space.

Dr. Goddard wanted to continue building rockets, but he was finding they were costing him more than he earned. He needed more money for supplies. So he sent a report, telling what he had done in rocket research and what he hoped to do, to scientific foundations. The Smithsonian Institution in Washington responded with a $5000 grant. But just when he had received his grant, World War I began. Dr. Goddard volunteered to investigate rockets as possible weapons. But the war ended before his work was put to use.

1918 · DR. GODDARD DEMONSTRATES HIS "BAZOOKA" TO THE ARMY

After the War, Dr. Goddard returned to his research. Now, more than ever, inventing a vehicle for outer space was the core of his being. As new ideas came to him, he added them to his report on the fundamentals of rocketry. Then on January 11, 1920, the Smithsonian published his report which was called "A Method of Reaching Extreme Altitudes." In the final section, Dr. Goddard mentioned how rockets could get to the moon. This created an unexpected sensation! Nine days later, headlines across the country were screaming the news that Dr. Goddard was working on a moon rocket. Dr. Goddard did not welcome the publicity. Though he clearly stated that he had not yet built a high altitude rocket of any kind, reporters continued to hound him for news of the moon flight. Letters and calls came from people everywhere, volunteering to be the first to land on the moon. Scheming real estate agents offered land on the moon for sale. Worst of all, Dr. Goddard found he had to defend his theories to science critics who called him a "crackpot" who had been struck by "moon madness." Disgusted, he withdrew from further publicity and went back to his independent research.

1920 · REPORTERS HOUND DR. GODDARD ABOUT HIS ROCKET REPORT

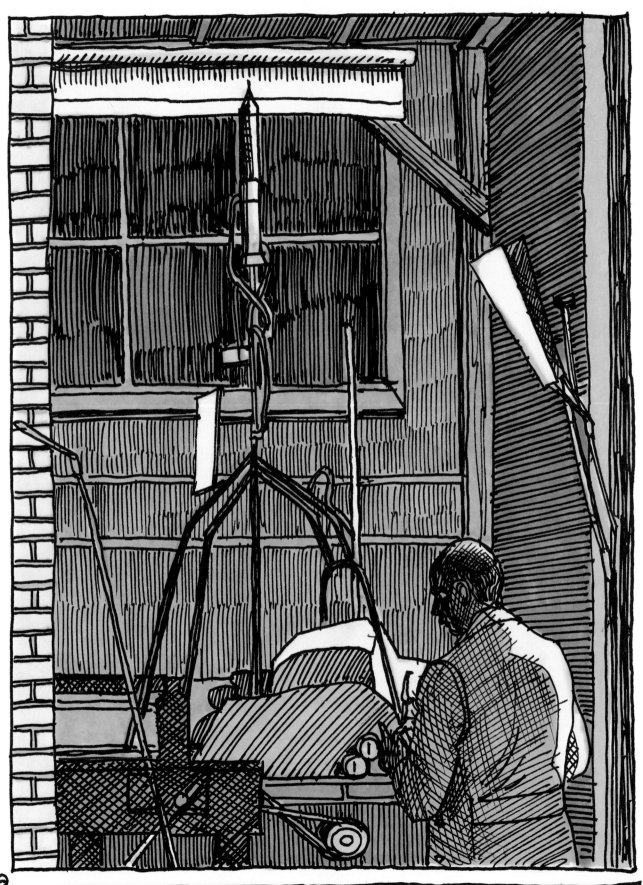

1920-25 • DR. GODDARD SETS TO WORK ON A LIQUID-FUEL ROCKET

Out of the public eye, Dr. Goddard kept trying to find a way to make a liquid-fuel rocket. Like a good yankee trader, he went shopping around chemical plants, hoping to find the fuels he needed. At last he found a chemical manufacturer who was producing liquid oxygen as a by-product of another chemical. The door to opportunity was open! True, Dr. Goddard still did not have the liquid hydrogen he wanted, but at least he had the necessary liquid oxygen, which he could combine with regular gasoline instead. Now he could begin building a liquid-fuel rocket. But it was not going to be an easy thing to do. It would have a host of problems attached to it. No longer was it enough to have a simple tube filled with powder like the solid-fuel rockets of the past. A liquid-fuel rocket had to have tanks for the oxygen and the gasoline. There had to be a special firing chamber in which the burning of the fuels took place. The oxygen tank had to be especially strong, since liquid oxygen will stay liquid only under high pressure and is apt to blow up into its gaseous state at any time. There had to be pumps to bring the two liquids to the firing chamber, and some sort of ignition to start things going. There had to be valves of several kinds. All of this would take many long hours and many years to hopefully develop and perfect.

Dr. Goddard experimented for more than five years to develop his liquid-fuel rocket. During that time he married his secretary, Esther Kisk. As well as being a loving wife, Esther worked as her husband's assistant, photographer, and accountant. She too had become a rocket buff. And Dr. Goddard supported his wife's needs, too. He helped her to attain her own dream of going to college and receiving a degree.

At last Dr. Goddard achieved a rocket that was ready for a test flight. On March 16, 1926, accompanied by his wife and two assistants, he took the rocket to an open field on the farm of a distant relative, Aunt Effie Ward. Mrs. Goddard got her camera ready to take motion pictures of the event. All were eager to know whether the rocket would overcome its own weight and rise in the air.

1926 · DR. GODDARD'S LIQUID-FUEL ROCKET IS SET UP FOR A TEST

Dr. Goddard and his assistants filled the tanks at the rear of the rocket with gasoline and liquid oxygen. They checked the two pipes, each about five feet long, that would send the gasoline and lox to the tiny rocket engine. Then Dr. Goddard ignited the engine with a blowtorch attached to a long pole. There was a tremendous blast as the gasoline and lox erupted. The rocket surged upward out of its launching stand. It climbed into the air. The world's first liquid-fuel rocket had made its first successful flight!

Dr. Goddard's rocket climbed to an altitude of 41 feet and covered an overall distance of 184 feet before it fell back to earth. Though it was not much of a performance by today's standards, the secret launching marked the beginning of modern rocketry. For that reason alone, the flight of the world's first successful liquid-fuel rocket was a historic triumph, comparable to the Wright Brothers' first airplane flight that led the world into the Air Age.

1926 · THE LAUNCHING OF THE WORLD'S FIRST LIQUID·FUEL ROCKET

While the world remained unaware that history had been made on a Massachusetts farm, Dr. Goddard went on to build and to test entirely new rockets. The fourth of these liquid-fuel rockets was launched on July 17, 1929. This launching did not go unnoticed. The rocket rose 90 feet and traveled 171 feet before crashing to the ground. The roar was heard two miles around. Fire trucks, police cars, and reporters arrived on the scene. Everyone was sure a plane had crashed. But when the emergency crews and reporters saw what had really happened, Dr. Goddard's name was in the news again. Headlines claimed he was now experimenting with a rocket to the moon.

This time Dr. Goddard was happy to have publicity, because the news of his rocket experiments came to the attention of Charles Lindbergh, the world-famous aviator and America's hero. Lindbergh arranged for a large grant for the rocket scientist from the Guggenheim Foundation. Now Dr. Goddard had money to set up a full-fledged rocket research center in Roswell, New Mexico. And just in time, too: the Smithsonian's money had run out and as a result of the last launching, Dr. Goddard was forbidden to fire any more rockets in the State of Massachusetts!

1929 · EMERGENCY CREWS RUSH TO THE SCENE OF THE FOURTH LAUNCHING

1935 · DR. GODDARD'S ROCKETS BREAK THE SOUND BARRIER

By the mid-1930's, the New Mexico workshop and launching tower were known throughout the world, as Dr. Goddard launched liquid-fuel rockets which attained speeds greater than that of sound and soared to 7500 feet and beyond. By then, however, he was no longer the only pioneer in liquid-fuel rockets. Space travel and rocket societies in the Soviet Union, Germany, the Netherlands, and Great Britain, as well as the United States, were now building and launching experimental liquid-fuel rockets of their own. By the end of World War II, Germany had introduced a secret weapon called the V-2, which was to lead the world directly into the Space Age. But even this rocket was built using the basic principles that Dr. Goddard had patented. There simply was no other way to build rockets to outer space.

Dr. Goddard did not live to see man land on the moon. He died in 1945, after a serious operation. After his death, he received many honors, and numerous prizes and awards were established in his name. In addition, the United States paid the Guggenheim Foundation and Mrs. Goddard $1,000,000 for the use of Dr. Goddard's 214 patents, which cover nearly every phase of modern rocketry. And Dr. Goddard's genius lives on. Today's rocket scientists carry on his dream as they send rockets to Mars and beyond, build space shuttles, and draw up plans for colonies in space.

HOW TO BUILD A MODEL SPACE ROCKET

- 1 paper towel tube
- 1 3″ long pencil
- 1 pen with pocket clip
- Scotch tape
- white glue
- 1 heavy duty rubber band at least 2½″ long by ¼″ wide
- 3 sheets of paper towels or 1 sheet of newspaper

- sharp scissors
- pencil, paper, carbon paper
- white flour paste made from ½ cup of flour and about one cup of water
- poster paints, brushes
- ice cream sticks (optional)

Trace or copy patterns. Put carbon paper under your drawing and retrace nose cone on one end of tube and the nozzle on the other. Cut out pieces along the tracing line.

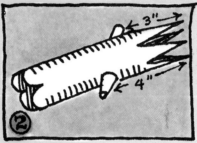

Make a small hole 3″ from the top of the nose cone with scissors. Make another hole opposite the first and 4″ from the top of the nose cone. Poke pencil through holes and glue.

Fold nose cone points together and tape. Soak small pieces of paper towel or newspaper in bowl of flour paste, then cover the rocket with the paper. Let dry.

Cut one inch wide streamers from a towel or newspaper to represent escaping gases. Glue the streamer ends just inside the rocket nozzle. Paint your rocket model and the streamers.

To send your rocket skyward, attach rubber band to pen clip and to pencil point on rocket. Pull pen to stretch rubber band while holding nozzle with other hand. Let go of nozzle and—zip!

To display model, fold out nozzle tabs and let the rocket rest on them. You may also want to build a launching tower. Build it with blocks or with ice cream sticks glued together.

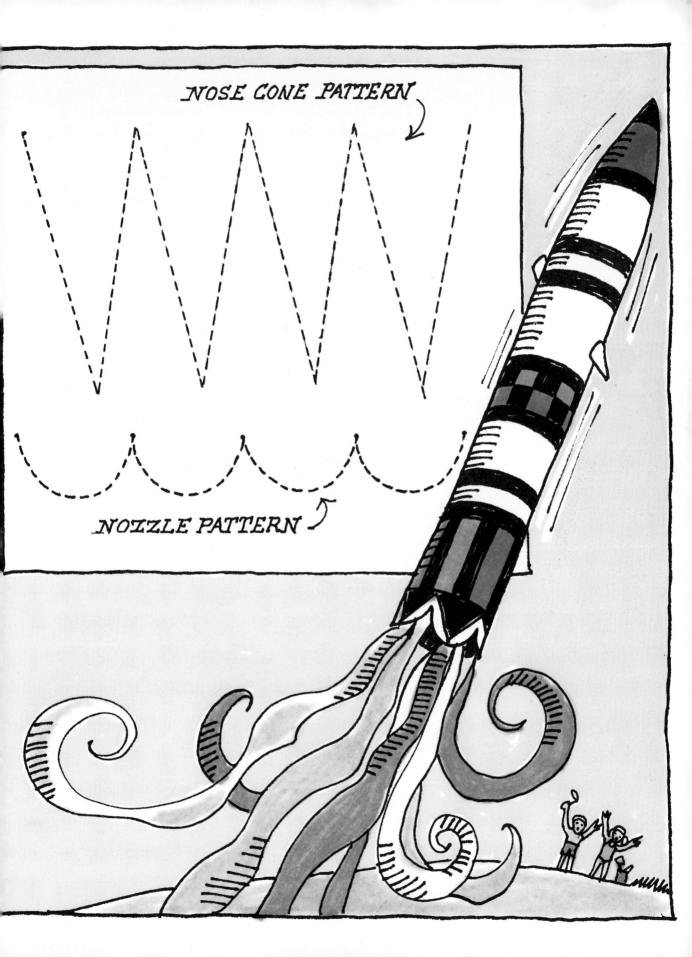

HOW A ROCKET WORKS

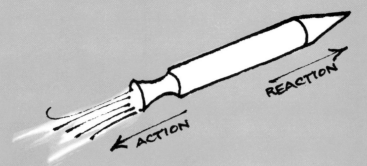

A rocket does not fly, as many people think. Instead, it is pushed forward through the atmosphere or space. This happens because a hot stream of gases, flowing backward from the nozzle, pushes the rocket forward. The principles of rocket flight that were worked out by Dr. Goddard were based on a law of physics formulated by Sir Isaac Newton in the seventeenth century. Newton's *Third Law of Motion* states that to every action there is an equal and opposite reaction. If you've seen movies of a cannon firing, you know how this works. When the cannon is fired, you see it kick back against the ground. This kick, or recoil, is the "reaction" of the cannon to the forward motion or "action" of the cannon ball. In the same manner, the forward motion of the rocket is the reaction to the backward motion.

Most modern space rockets use liquid fuel. The fuel itself is usually kerosene, gasoline, or alcohol, and it is combined with liquid oxygen (lox) as the oxidizer to make the fuel burn. These propellants are stored in separate tanks in front of the rocket engine and are forced into the combustion chamber by pumps or compressed gas. The fuel is mixed with the liquid oxygen in the combustion (burning) chamber and burns at very high temperatures when ignited. This creates hot gases that rush out the nozzle, causing the rocket to move forward. Soon, just as Dr. Goddard perceived, rockets will use electrical and atomic propulsion for space travel. Dr. Goddard was already experimenting with ion propulsion for rockets before he died in 1945.

No rocket can stay up for more than a few minutes. When it has reached the peak of its flight, it plunges back to earth. Even the most explosive of today's liquid fuels are not powerful enough to send a single-stage rocket beyond the earth's atmosphere. Therefore, for a rocket to soar to outer space, it must be a step, or multistage, vehicle—one with several rockets mounted one on top of another. With this type, when the fuel of each rocket is burnt up, the next one is set off and will soar faster than ever. To protect the people on the ground, each burnt-out rocket will explode and tear into tiny fragments as it begins to fall. The last rocket will not fall. It will be traveling too fast for the earth to pull it back.

THE WORLD'S SPACE JOURNEYS TODAY